SCINTILLATING MUSINGS

SCINTILLATING MUSINGS

Reena Samyal Rathore

Highbrow Scribes Publications
New Delhi

Published : 2022
ISBN : 978-81-949062-8-5

Published by
Highbrow Scribes Publications
55-C, Jhang Appts., Sec.-13
Rohini, New Delhi - 110085
Mobile : +91-8826398333
+91-7982333488
E-mail : highbrowscribes@gmail.com
Website : www.highbrowscribes.com

Typeset by: Shagun Graphics, Delhi-110086

Printed by APAC Business Solutions Pvt. Ltd., New Delhi

Introduction

Scintillating musings are my personal moments of spark which motivated me to pen down feelings reverberating inside me. These were not only moments of joy, but also admiration, faith, strength, hope, veneration, compassion, pain, anguish that I wish to communicate with the outside world. My endeavour is to be able to create a repository of reverence which as a soul-mate, friend, mother, wife and above all, a responsible society member one undergoes.

We, as social beings, are connected by a sentimental relationship that is the bond which my set of poems are crafted to strengthen and have therapeutic effects on the readers' minds.

The theme of these poems is the expressions of diverse emotions which have been communicated by a lover, joyous coursemates, nature lover, a dreamer and above all, a kid at heart.

The poems depict my sensitivity speculated not only from my personal experiences but also from those around me. My earnest endeavour has been to make compositions more rational, pure and lasting in their expression.

CONTENTS

Tribute
and
Salute

TRUE SOLDIER

A black day so we may call,

when a valiant soldier on the soil had a fall

with a bullet that pierced his heart

and brutally divided it into two parts;

One for his motherland he had preserved,

One for his family's dreams he had reserved.

Now everything is futile;

Prayers and mourning for a while.

The brave soldier has left on an operation unknown,

His soul has left his body and flown.

Not even passed the two score mark in his life.

Wasn't he too young to have left his family, his beloved wife?

While defending his nation's pride,

Couldn't he become a little selfish and take his family's side?

No, he could not have done so

because he was a true soldier to the core.

A deep void that he has left behind

can never be filled by words no matter how kind!!

All that remains are some sweet and sour memories;

A box full of albums, uniforms, shoes, files, some answers and some queries....

"Pupa we were happy when we heard the news that you were coming home....

Till we saw that you were wrapped in the tricolour, kept in a wooden box and had to be flown.....!!"

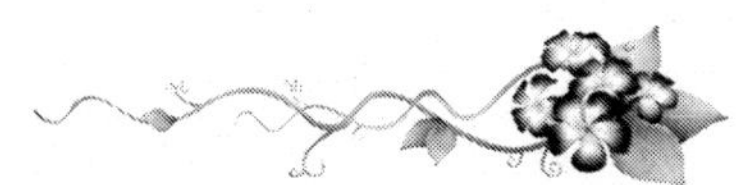 3 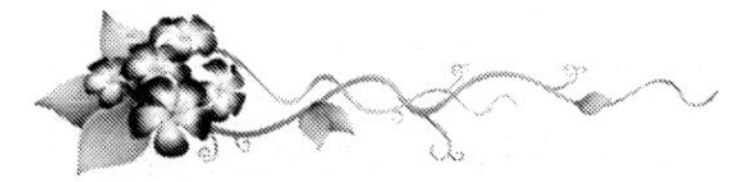

@PULWAMA ATTACK

#RIPBRAVEHEARTS..

What started as a great day

ended on such a sad note.

Red hearts everywhere made everyone believe and say

that love is for real and not just part of any quote......

Love for family, love for friends, love for siblings;

Today was a day of celebration of love for all human beings.

But alas! All the love was overcast, by clouds of anguish, by afternoon

when the media surfaced with the bitter news soon......

The news that revealed that the world is no more a place for love and humanity,

People surely have lost all their senses and sanity!!

Such cold-blooded murder

surely makes one shudder,

throats getting choked,

questions getting evoked.

It's not about 1, 2 or 30;

It's about how many more?

It's not about the game of politics often so dirty;

It's about the anxious mother who continuously looks at the door....

.... probably waiting to see her son very soon.

Wasn't he her biggest strength and boon....

sent from the One above.....

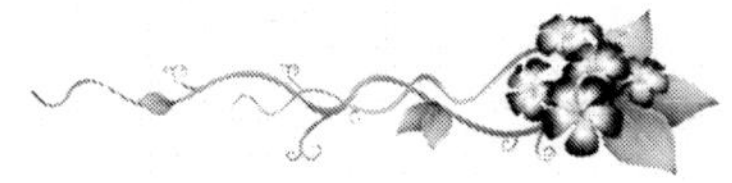 4 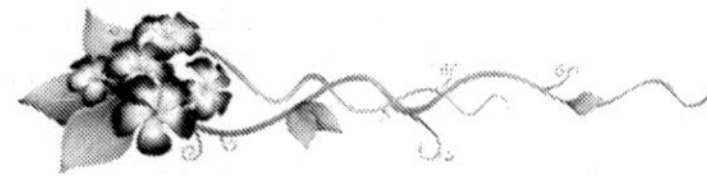

To whom she had nurtured with nothing but pure love?

Or it's about a wife / girlfriend whom he just texted valentine's messages
including one that read that he will love her unconditionally in all ages?

Or it's about a younger sister
who was waiting for a present from her dear brother?

Or it's about all his friends
who are waiting for him to spend with him a great weekend?

Or it's about an old father
who will shoulder his son's bier and light his pyre?

Or it's about the ground where the bloodstains remain

The soil also asks shamelessly how much more blood do I need to sustain?

The Sky God's pouring heavily

Or, is it the hearts of the martyrs sighing sadly....?

"We sacrificed to keep the others safe and sound.

But alas! Our numbers have decreased on the ground!!"

How long will it take for issues to get resolved?

How long will it take to get the militancy problem solved?

How long will the Forces continue to extend a helping hand?

How long will the brave Patriots be shooed away from their own motherland?

How long will the stone-pelters think that they are a part of the freedom struggle?

How long from across the borders will the idiots continue to smuggle ammunition and
hatred in abundance?

How long on the tunes of satanic and insane morons will the foolish people continue to
dance?

THE SOLDIER'S PILGRIMAGE

He darts to reach the lofty peak

carrying the holy tricolour with pride

in a weather pious and not so bleak

with his comrades by his side!

Clothes dampened with pure blood and sweat

after winning the battle so hard!

Now is the time not to regret

for his enemies' plans had been marred!

While he scurried to reach the destination:

Not a shadow dared to make him stop.

He marched on with determination

to be there atop!

Alas! Many would not know

the saga of his glory & courage.

But on this path does he care-a big NO!

For he was on a patriotic pilgrimage......!!!!!

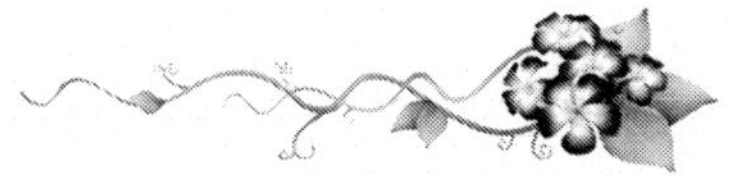 7 

URI

Today the heart bleeds

for a consoling balm, it pleads.

Again some more lost their life

leaving behind their old parents, kids
and wife,

leaving them with promises many

Alas! Failed to fulfil, due to destiny.

Left on an unknown terrain. The valiant
nineteen

scaled many heights but this they had
never seen.

They move on right out of deep slumber,

caught in gunshots and their burning
bunker.

They are not the soldiers but the
nineteen 'Whys'.

No strategies, no talks, no prayers -
their life nothing can buy;

How many more? An answer to this is
sought.

How many more in such cowardly acts
will get caught?

Once the joyous valley harvested saffron
gold,

is depressed with stories of many of
these, that'll forever remain untold.

On their body and imprinted on their
soul was their identification number.

They lived and martyred like a true
soldier.

May you all be with the Almighty as His
inseparable parts!

Rest in Peace - the nineteen brave-hearts.

7TH DECEMBER 1996

25 years of glorious service to the
nation.
It's time for some jubilant
celebration.
25 years of being there
in normal situations and away from
the ones that wanted you to dare.
25 years of having seen it all
together
ever since you crossed the "Antim
Path" together.
Remembering all your comrades
who trained for almost 548 days
with you in sun and shade.
Over the years your beret changed
and so did your badges
as you went through your service's
different stages.
The changes chiselled you all into
fine officers of grit and valour.
You worked for the nation without
failure.
Today is a Day to remember your
mates who left so soon.
They are up there somewhere amidst
the stars and moon.
They stay forever in your heart.
Forever there as an inseparable part.
25 years of sharing happiness and
sorrow with each other -
this strong bond of comradeship
shall be carried forever and ever.

Glory
and
Worry

ELIXIR

The Rain God lifted his hand

how to give relief from the scorching heat he

had beautifully planned.

Dropped some showers of joy on the sand.

Little girls rejoiced and so did the naughty boys' band.

Farmers took their ploughs to prepare their land.

The pleasant change offered comfort to each sweat gland.

The shiny drops formed a chain as it dripped from the hair strand.

Pure elixir for the dry land!

Replenishing unbiasedly every mountain, forest, grassland.

People huddled under a shed at the bus stand.

Those at home enjoyed their favourite tea brand.

This selfless relation between the pearls from the sky and the thirsty earth is for all to understand.

It is a relation of sheer love and acceptance without any demand.

Reena

MIGHTY SUMMER

Resplendent spring gives way to the mighty summer -

a season of which I am not a great admirer.

Once upon a time, it was great fun

when we enjoyed vacations by playing in the sun.

But now summers mean unbearable heat and rage.

All thanks to the human race for bringing our earth to such a disastrous stage,

with air conditioners and coolers on the whole day,

making kids hardly want to go out and play.

It brings along irritating insects and epidemic diseases.

The dry, hot and sweaty weather makes our clothes unkempt with dirt and creases.

It's a season when people are louder in their conversation.

It's a season to get soaked in perspiration.

Season when streams go dry;

Season when gentle plants wither and die;

Unbearable heat, unbearable attitude

Makes me long for a visit to a cooler destination with peace and solitude.

THE FIERY NATURE

The nature is ready to give it back

what we have offered it over the years.

The colour of the future seems black

and the pre-dominant emotion shall be fear.

The waves that once brought the pearls on the beach

are ready to throw only plastic cans and litter.

The nature is all set to preach....preach

Sermons that are so harsh and bitter.

The mountains are sliding to turn into uneven plains.

The fertile plains are transforming into deserts dry.

The Sky God's wrath in the form of devastating rains

takes many a lives and leaves many others to moan and cry.

Once shamelessly, we sowed the chemical seeds

and the nature gets the privilege to make us eat

the most dangerously toxic feed

though injected with venomous syrups so sweet.

The time has come when the nature will give it all back.

Not in a bit but in heaps of what we gave it.

It's time to increase our levels of concern that we may at times lack

for nature now is no more going to forgive and forget.

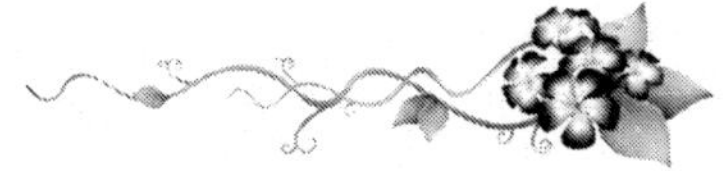 14 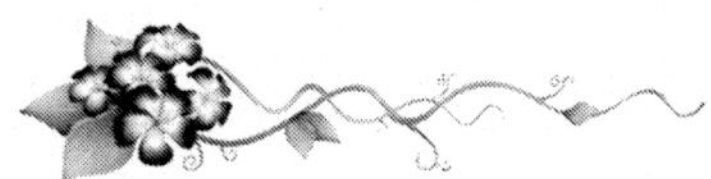

WELCOME WINTER

It's a partial cold morning

announcing that winter is knocking -

Get up and get going,

Feel the cool breeze for which all through summers you've been longing....

Every creature seems to be cheering.

When the wintry air is caressing

and causing a sudden shudder.

Although not so harsh to make them shiver....

There is a peaceful whiteness in the day.

The bright orangeness of the Sun has suddenly faded away.

Wrap yourself with a warm cover,

Sit outside and make nature your lover.

Enjoy this moment with a rejuvenating hot cup of tea

or take a large sip of an aromatic coffee.

SPRING TIME

It's Spring time

that makes the surroundings
pristine.

Our feathered friends
chirping on the grapevine,

the bees humming songs
pure and divine,

the flowers joyously face the
sun,

watching them bloom and
stretch is so much fun.

The insects crawling on the
ground,

feeding on the fallen leaves
without any sound,

the bushes are thick and
green again,

the air is clean as if washed
by the rain,

the butterflies fluttering to
collect their nectar,

the feeling of freshness and
joy everywhere.

I LOVE WINTER'S SNOW MUCH!

I am madly in love with the winter season

for I have all the reason

to stay in the bed till late.

As everything is ice cold, right from the slippers till the gate....

I have a reason not to jog

as the air is thick with all the fog...

Time to burn calories with all the steam; while taking a bath

because no more I want to tread on that cold cemented path....

The biggest challenge for the day

is how to throw that cosy quilt away...

Hot ginger tea is welcome any time of the day.

'No' to it, I would dare not say!

The day is not washed in the golden hue.

There is whiteness spread all over like a sheet that's brand new....

The chirpiness of the birds is a little less!

But it's a treat to watch them cuddle in their small nest....

It's time for hot soups, Christmas cake, lots of lotions and creams

It's time for colourful wool, fireplace and lots of dreams...

Hugs are spread in abundance now.

They surely make you warm, don't know how!

Love everything about the wintry winter chill

as I watch it through the window with my cup of coffee on the sill!!!

 17 

Sky
is the
Limit !

GATHER YOURSELF!!!

Our past is an experience: Our future a mystery:

Remembering the sorrows of the yester tense

and carrying it like a note in today's diary;

It is the biggest blunder of the time

that spoils even your present in its prime.

The scars of the past like an evening shadow

at dawn must on their own disappear

and not leave their impression for others to know,

for they would not understand the how, when and where

they should be carried in the mind like a guiding light

showing way in the darkness of life and making it bright.

Their intensity will increase for sure

if kept locked in the heart as a priceless treasure.

Let them answer all your queries

And not become a source of your new days' worries.

They are just a speck in the universe's totality.

Don't be disheartened by their intensity;

Like a changing season, they would pass on their own.

Realise that many more have gone through this phase and eventually grown..
You can see the beads of your life as a scatter

but with a positive attitude, you can create a new necklace that's even better,

Get up and take your life in your stride.

Don't spoil your today's joy just because yesterday you cried!!

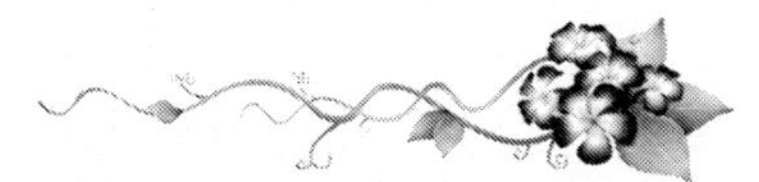

RISE TO BE WISE

Rise, fall and rise!

And be wiser.

Risen, fallen and risen!

Mature like a wine that has aged over many a season.

Smile, cry and smile!

And make this life worthwhile.

Smiling, crying and smiling!

Empty your heart with all that is piling.

Start, end and start!

Even if it tears your heart.

Starting, ending and starting!

It's all about experimenting.

Repair, tear and repair!

Will teach you lessons on how to take care.

Repairing, tearing and repairing!

Believe in hoarding love and also sharing.

The success of your life depends on how you sail through it all

And rise even if you've had a real bad fall.

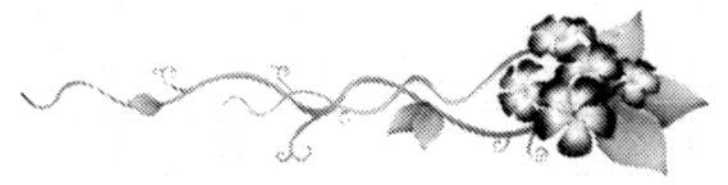 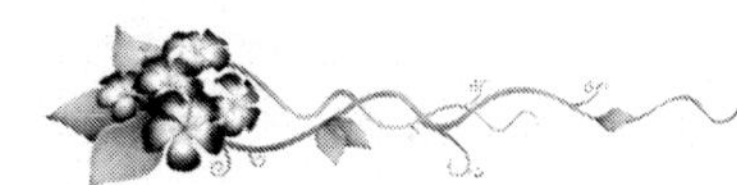

SHADES OF LIFE

Some things in life put you down.
Sometimes all you do is sit and frown.
Sometimes it feels uneasy to even wear a crown.
Sometimes the world looks so dull and brown.....
That is the time to realise your worth;
That is the time to celebrate your birth;
That is the time to pat your back;
That is the time not to let your heart break and crack.....

A temporary phase that it is!
Though gives you pain and makes your forehead crease;
Remember not to let your dreaming cease.
This too shall pass if you let it please.....
Just like a dew drop on a grass blade,
Memories of disdain and sorrow will also fade
for life is all about the Sun and its shade.
Always believe that for something special you were made......!!!!

SOMETIMES.....!!!

Sometimes minor things affect us so
much
that we forget to see our major aim.

Sometimes we get so disturbed by the
slush
that we forget to see the benefits of the
rain.

Sometimes scolding from our parents hurt
us to the core
that we forget to appreciate their sacrifice.

Sometimes in our quest for having more
we forget to use our own things
that are nice.

Sometimes we want to sing a perfect song
that we forget to hum sweet lullabies.

Sometimes we want to become so strong
that we forget to wipe the tears of a child
who cries.

Sometimes it's all about our wants and
longings in life
that we forget to lend a helping hand.

Sometimes we want to climb that unseen
ladder
that we forget to make a disabled on his
feet stand!!

But Sometimes we must notice all the
reasons
that we have to smile and spread joy all
around

and sometimes we must not forget to
listen to our own heart's sound!!!!!

Familia

A DAY SANS WOMEN

The dishes unclean;
the brass sans sheen;
the unkempt hair of children;
the garden's all barren;
the laundry all scattered;
the flour and eggs waiting to be battered;
Vessels all empty;
Stomachs ain't happy!!
Schools without students!
Patients without attendants!
Untidy rooms,
Untouched brooms,
Sandals without heels,
Fruits with intact peels,
Dictionary loses the word 'beauty'!!
Man loses all sanity;
No more emotions and no more feelings;
No more whistles and no more hearts fluttering;
Empty cradles rocking!!
Would it be a day worth living?
Pamper the WOMAN who pampers you the most
who inspite of slogging whole day by evening becomes a perfect host
in good times and bad.
The one who smiles just for you even when she is sad!!
Appreciate the one who strives to make your life comfortable
because without her, sorry to say, life would be unthinkable!!

TRANSFER OF LOVE

Daughters are indeed special!
You realize their worth only when they leave.
They have a heart that's palatial
and loads of unconditional love that they give
to their parents and siblings
which can be termed as 'The Best Offering'.
A love that is pious and pure
that over the ages increases for sure.
I wish there was some way to hold the time forever
so that they would leave us never.
I, as a daughter, want to go to my mother's lap again
and get shielded by her during storm and rain.
The most comforting words were 'hers'
which I could never get to listen again in years........
To think that my daughter is my seed
and me of my mother's indeed.
A transfer of love from yesterday to today and then to tomorrow
surely gives immense happiness and curbs all sorrow......

THE WORLD IS SO BLACK!!!

O Mother! Why did you make me blind

and brought me into a world that is so black and unkind?

For me, colours mean the hues of black and knowledge of Blue, Green, Yellow, Red, White I lack.

I know my world is now based on what I hear!

Only from that I come to know of the dangers far and near.

Although you describe me everything in the best possible way,

I want to see them to know if they are as beautiful as you say.

I want to see you the first and foremost

because without you in this world - I am completely lost.

And I know you love me the most,

that is why for my treatment you run from pillar to post.

Shapes, colours and faces are all a feeling for me. A feeling, that is too deep inside, that no one else can see.

Unlike other children, their first landmark

for growth is running to you with a cheerful smile,

For me, it is counting my steps to reach a hard solid part of a building and being agile.

I have been told to turn off the power switches as I pass through the corridor

Although that is just an exercise and nothing more.

My movements are restricted!

My happiness is calculated!

My books are outd`ated!

My future is speculated!

Why did you let this happen to me,

O! Mother?

Why can't I be like my brother?

Do you know how difficult it is to stay in a world that is only black?

But then, any way, this is better than staying in a colourful world

with insensitive people who care for others lack!

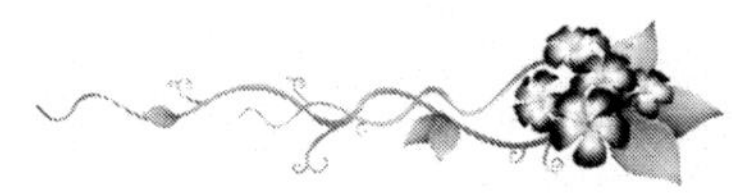 

"DREAMS"

Some things come in life as a surprise;

Kids are one such prize.

But when did those dreamy castles fade away?

(Which were made of rosy petals and had a life that was happy and gay).

Are kids a compensation for that ideal vision?

Or are they for their disappearance the main reason?

Earlier there was a desire to see those dreams come true.

Today there is a desire to see dreams for the kids that are new...

Is all this worth the sacrifice?

Wanting to see a future for the kids that is nice?

The truth is that life is a full circle.

Our parents gave up their desires without a crinkle.

They gave us the comfort to dream,

whether we accomplished them or they just flowed away like a stream.

The same comfort to our kids we must give

to encourage them to have entirely new dreams to help them live.

They are indeed the main reason for our living

so pass on the dreams to them as your best offering.

NOSTALGIA

I miss the wonderful days of my childhood

when my play included toys made from plastic and wood.

When the bubbles of soap displayed colours so vibrant

and catching them quickly seemed so important.

When throwing tantrums and crying was my armour

and the frequently visited place was the ice-cream parlor.

When imitating my teacher at birthday parties,

was a thing of pride.

Not to forget eating those yummy chocolate pastries

and enjoying those giant wheel rides.

When wearing those high heels of my mother,

draping her silk sarees in front of the mirror

and trying to style those tresses

transferred me into a world of dreams making me a promising actress.

Whenever I would watch those cartoons,

I would burst into peals of laughter.

My room was always filled with golden balloons

which dad would bring for his loving daughter.

Miss those days of long hours of play and fun

when grass was a carpet and a twisted stick a gun.

When mistakes were committed out of innocence

and the biggest crime was jumping over the fence.

Wish I could go back to that time again

and re-live those moments of sheer joy and no pain.

Place I Belong

QUINTESSENTIAL WORLD

There is a magical world within the bricked fence

extraordinaire with undefiled roads and foliage so dense

aerated by the well-strained air;

on and off overcast by clouds with God's rays so fair.

The environment resonates with the clattering of the blabber bird

and not to miss the dumbly moving blue cow's herd;

The mysterious and challenging trekking trail

sauntering on its complete length; I often fail

the edifices made of bricks and concrete

made more magnificent by the force so elite.

Behold the sight of the marching troops,

well-coordinated steps and uniformed breathing rhythm even while in groups.

The alley of well-spaced trees

on both sides converging to form prominent V's;

The extravagant peacocks add vibrancy all around

the fragrant plumeria rooted gracefully on the ground.

A world that everyone would want to be in!

A world soaring with courage and joy from within......

 31 

LET THE SOUL DANCE

I stroll on the wet grey path

cleansed by nature's soothing bath;

with the dust settled for the time being

and the cuckoos on the boughs gleefully sing.

The exquisite colours of the peacock's feather

look more vibrant due to the weather

with the freshness of the air

and the sky so fair.

The world seems drenched in happiness galore.

Sends my way windy invites from under my door

calls out to let the sorrows of yesterday

for a while give way

to the abundant blessings

that the nature is daily offering

and let the soul dance and rejoice

on the songs sung by wind in its pleasing voice.

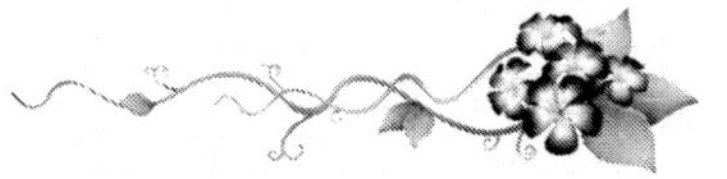 32 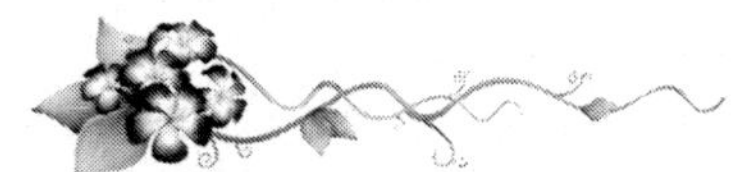

RIGMAROLE OF MOVING AND PACKING

Happy, happy!

Going to a new place.

Open, open!

Boxes excitedly at a fast pace.

Set, set!

For the stuff find a suitable place.

Explore, explore!

As you have already set your base.

Buy, buy!

All that's a speciality of the new place.

Spend, spend!

On buying some more things that attract your race.

Rejoice, rejoice!

New purchases bring a bright smile on the face.

Use, use!

And gather loads of compliments and praise.

Suddenly, suddenly!

Time to move to another place.

Packing, packing!

Here you stand confused and dazed.

New things, new things!

Filling them in the boxes becomes a challenging maze.

Create, create!

Buy new boxes to make some more space.

Two years, two years!

The saga continues and ends only after the retirement days.

MY LAND – A BESTOWER

My pride my India,

the Seventh largest by area,

with the most populous democracy,

with its rich cultural and lingual diversity...............

A nation that we call our mother,

where different religious beliefs thrive together.

A nation that gave the world Takshashila University,

a nation where numeral 'Zero' got its true identity...............

The chess game earlier-known 'Chaturanga' originated in this land,

ornamental buttons were also created here from sea shells on the sand,

alternative medicine Ayurveda cured many a beings.

We not only gave to the world Cashmere wool but many other things..............

Yoga still continues to keep people fit and fine,

a nation that is meant to always grow and shine,

With the grand Tajmahal the wondrous wonder,

the Tourists are enchanted by its architectural grandeur.

As our nation celebrates its 75th year of Independence,

I bow my head in respect and admiration for its magnificence..................

GOLDILOCKS

As I stroll on the campus road,
inviting me is the avenue of
Laburnum Gold.
I stop for a while to admire the golden
chain,
the flowers hanging like drops of rain.
The trees that seem to have been
touched by King Midas,
Goldilocks of the plant, world famous
for their golden yellow flowers.
Their plumate leaves gleefully hold
the treasure,
gazing at them is a sheer pleasure.
Some of my fondest childhood
memories revolve
around this golden shower tree,
but its thick juicy smell still makes me
a wee bit dizzy.
In the soaring temperature with its
pendulous inflorescence of canary
yellow,
it becomes conspicuous against the
blue sky above and the grey soil
below
intrudes any seemingly dull and
inanimate environ,
bringing it to life like a welcome siren.
As I watch them stand in silence like
a group of saints meditating
for a while, I too am left quiescent
almost hallucinating......!!!!!